JAPAN
The Four Seasons

JAPAN

The Four Seasons

Johnny Hymas

SHUFUNOTOMO CO., LTD.

I dedicate this book to the poetry of nature,
for without her never-ending verse
man cannot survive.

Book design by Toshiaki Suzuki

Johnny Hymas Office
4274 Minami Yamada-cho
Tsuzuki-ku, Yokohama City
Kanagawa Prefecture
Japan 224
Tel. & Fax: 81-45-593-0059

First printing, 1990
Sixth printing, 1997

Published by Shufunotomo Co., Ltd.
2-9, Kanda Surugadai, Chiyoda-ku
Tokyo, 101 Japan

Printed in Japan

ISBN4-07-975411-6

Foreword

Johnny Hymas and I have much in common. We were both born in parts of Britain noted for their fiercely proud local identities. He was born in Yorkshire; I in Wales. Then we both went to school in counties rich in beautiful, gentle pastoral scenery and well-preserved historical sights. He went to school in Worcestershire; I in the neighboring county of Gloucestershire. We both know well the lovely green hills of the Cotswolds and the Malverns. In our youth, both of us did unusual jobs. He was a professional acrobat; I a professional wrestler. But the thing we have most in common is a deep love of Japan and a great concern for the country's future. His daughter, Hiromi, is fifteen, and my daughter, Alicia, is five. This marvelous country is their home.

Coming from Britain, a proud and scenic island country with a long history, we both find much in Japan to make us feel at home. We find Japan to be a treasure trove of natural wonders, a harmonious balance between the works of man and nature.

Johnny's pictures capture the extraordinary contrasts of this land. Maple and bamboo growing together. To us, this is remarkable indeed. Maple is a northern snow country tree, and bamboo is a plant of the tropics or semitropics. Japan has tiny terraced paddy fields like small perfect emeralds. Paddies so small

Japanese farmers joke that they may lose one when they lay their straw raincoat on the ground. Japan is a land of ancient Shinto shrines and Buddhist temples whose forms and colours blend perfectly with nature. This archipelago has sea ice in the north and coral in the south. Despite her fierce martial tradition, Japan is a safe and friendly country. Travellers can go anywhere freely, without fearing personal violence or encountering blatant dishonesty.

Although Johnny and I come from a land we love and are both proud of, we love Japan and her people even more. And we worry that some of what we love most about Japan is being lost. Beautiful landscapes are disappearing at a pace that takes our breath away. I hope this book will nudge people into thinking about what a lovely land this is, and what a shame it would be if this natural scenery were lost for future generations.

The photographs here reflect the beauty and depth of love for nature that we both want to believe still characterize the Japanese people. We continue to believe that the majority of Japanese yearn for lasting harmony with nature, and wholeheartedly desire the preservation of their natural heritage from the folly of man's rampant pollution.

Eight years of labor and love went into compiling these photographs. I hope they will touch the heart of everyone who looks at them, and inspire a renewed dedication to preserve and nurture not only the exquisite beauty of this land but all lands.

From one nature lover to another... well done!

C.W. Nicol
Kurohime, Nagano, 1990

Introduction

There is nothing ugly; I never saw an ugly thing in my life; for let the form of an object be what it may, light, shade and perspective will always make it beautiful.

—John Constable 1776–1837

The rain on a simple blade of grass, the silent trails on mountain peaks, never-ending waves breaking upon the shores, a bamboo thicket rustled by an aimless wind, a rising sun above a sea of clouds, the moon so near and yet so far.

These visual sensations—their texture, timbre, shape and weight—the precious treasures and inexhaustible riches of na-ture and her ever-changing moods are the themes of my life and work.

The first light breaks on a red hori-zon. In the foreground, vapours eddy across a primeval marshland. Waiting with camera poised and senses taut—the shutter clicks. The fleeting moment is frozen as it passes into time, gone forever, never to return.

This is but one phase in the compli-cated interaction between nature in motion and the task of trying to capture it with my lenses. The seasons manifest themselves with an undying persistence; they wait for no one. Their flow is precise and compelling. My camera, film, and self are but worthless objects against the awesomeness of nature's vital functions—we are just crude, simple tools that at chosen moments are able to record the abstract fantasies and fickle moods of the phenomenon we call nature. For me, this constant metamorphosis is mysterious and dramatic and I never tire of pointing my camera in its direction.

I use an old, weatherbeaten, oft-dropped Hasselblad camera and Carl Zeiss lenses, which have been the tools of my trade for twenty-five years. I feel comfortable with their touch and the way they react to my every whim. I would never part with these old friends, my companions in the wilderness. They help me capture the moods and fleeting moments for which I search. Manipulating such old familiar tools is of paramount importance when there are only split seconds to shoot swiftly changing landscapes.

My photographic expeditions have taken me all over the Japanese archipelago. Japan is a spectacularly beautiful country that captivated me almost from the moment I first arrived seventeen years ago. I have seen much of the country since then, and have developed a deep respect and understanding for the delicate beauty of its natural terrain.

When I am in the confines of my small tent, waiting for the dawn to break, I sometimes lie awake listening to the sounds of nature. Even in the dead of night, I have learned, each season tells its own story.

I listen to the grand silence of primeval forests whispering their warnings, I see oceans awash with the residue of man's greed, I hear the endless pitiful cries for help from a voiceless nature, I feel sadness and shame for the heedlessness of man.

Johnny Hymas
Tokyo, 1990

Acknowledgments

I wish to offer my sincere thanks to the following people who have helped me with this project...for their care and understanding.

Hiroshi Yasumura, Q Photo International, Inc., for his many years of efforts and assistance, and the Q Photo International staff; C. W. Nicol for writing the foreword; Jonathan Lloyd-Owen, Editor, *Intersect* magazine, and Anne Pepper, travel writer, for their editorial assistance; Shunichi Kamiya, Editor in Chief of the International Department of Shufunotomo Company, Ltd., whose support and encouragement made this project possible.

And my heartfelt love and thanks to my wife Yasuko and daughter Hiromi, who saw me through so many years of chasing the seasons.

SPRING

行く春や
鳥啼き魚の
目は泪　芭蕉

行燈を
とぼさず春を
惜しみけり　几董

春

Loathe to let spring go
Birds cry and even fishes'
Eyes are wet with tears.
　　　　　—Basho

Walking through the countryside in late
winter, when all is stark and bare, I come
across the first signs of awakening spring:
witch hazel burgeoning in a leafless forest;
narcissus flowers, oblivious to the elements,
blooming in a secluded glade; and just down
a winding trail, plum trees blossoming despite
a bitter north wind.

　　These early flowers tell us that below
ground a new birth has begun, and that we
are about to witness the magic of an unfold-
ing Japanese spring. Cherry, peach, apple,
azalea, quince, and rape—they will soon blossom forth in a riot of colours all over the land.

　　In tandem with these changes, *haru-
ichiban*—the first warm spring wind—gusts in
from the south. The balmy weather affects
young and old alike. They don their spring
attire to go dance, sing, and picnic beneath
the blossom-laden trees. Cherry blossom
season has arrived.

　　The cherry blossom is considered to be the
symbol of the samurai, because as they die,
cherry blossoms fall to the ground in their
prime, still proud and beautiful. The samurai,
too, even in their prime, regarded death as a
thing of great pride and beauty, and looked to
the cherry blossom as their inspiration.

　　A verse by Kito expresses not only the
sadness of a passing spring but for me, the
sadness I feel at the passing of all seasons.

Not daring to light the paper lantern
I grieved
For the fading spring.
　　　　　—Kito

Plum blossoms. The branches droop above the rustic
thatched-roof gate of Jindaiji Temple. Tsutsujigaoka, Tokyo.

Pink and white plum blossoms blend harmoniously
with a red shrine. Kitano Tenmangu, Kyoto.

Oze Plateau in early spring. The mountain trees are
reflected in the waters of the marsh. Fukushima Prefecture.

Mountain cherries and variegated colours of spring
adorn the steep banks of Lake Okutama, Tokyo.

White mountain cherry
trees grace the precipitous
slopes of Okutama, Tokyo.

Kodemari flowers veiled in the long shadows
of the setting sun. Tsutsujigaoka, Tokyo.

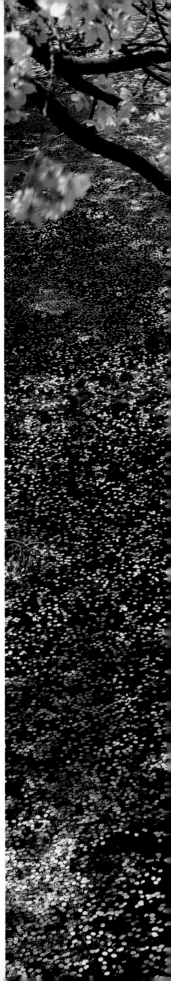

Fallen cherry blossoms
float on the quiet waters of
the moat at Hirosaki Castle.
Hirosaki, Aomori Prefecture.

A tunnel of cherry trees leads to the
entrance of an ancient Shinto shrine.
Kofu, Yamanashi Prefecture.

Urami waterfall surrounded by an irradiance of
spring foliage. Nikko City, Tochigi Prefecture.

Wild azaleas colour the slopes of Irohazaka. Nikko
National Park, Tochigi Prefecture.

Cherry in full bloom. The branches caress the roof
of Izusan Shrine. Atami City, Shizuoka Prefecture.

The five-storied pagoda of Saishoin Temple with
a large cherry tree blooming in the foreground.
Hirosaki City, Aomori Prefecture.

A fresh green maple reflects the brilliance of a spring day. Chichibu National Park, Saitama Prefecture.

A solitary cherry in full flower graces the mountain slopes of Hakone. Shizuoka Prefecture.

Mount Fuji seen across the waters of Lake Tanukiko at daybreak. Shizuoka Prefecture.

Shiraito Falls. The source of this famous waterfall originates beneath the slopes of Mount Fuji. Shizuoka Prefecture.

Oze Marsh blanketed with morning mist. On the
banks of a stream *mizu-basho*, or skunk cabbage,
signals the arrival of spring on the plateau.
Fukushima Prefecture.

Oirase River. Fresh spring trees stand in contrast
with the rugged rock face of a ravine. Towada,
Aomori Prefecture.

Japanese witch hazel heralds the very first days of
spring. Ogose, Saitama Prefecture.

A waterfall cascading from a rocky cleft in the
valley of Nishizawa. Mitomi Village,
Yamanashi Prefecture.

A field of rape flowers
thrives on the shores of
Lake Hokuryuko. Iiyama,
Nagano Prefecture.

The snaking waters of Kirifuri Falls loop
down the canyon of Kirifuri Plateau. Nikko
National Park, Tochigi Prefecture.

Luxuriant green and red maple leaves blend
delicately in a mountain thicket at Yoshino Village.
Nara Prefecture.

Iridescent leaves manifest a motif of spring.
Shosenkyo Ravine, Yamanashi Prefecture.

Oze Plateau. The aftermath
of a rainy day. A low-lying
mist partially shrouds the
distant mountain.
Fukushima Prefecture.

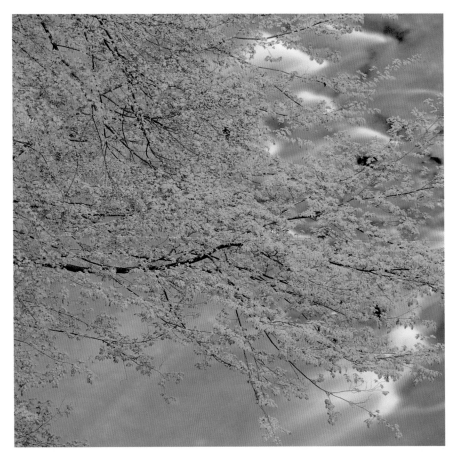

Branches of spring verdure overhang the
waters of Taba Ravine. Yamanashi Prefecture.

A droplet of water still clings to a Japanese quince flower after an April shower.
Mukojima Hyakkaen Garden, Tokyo.

Narcissus flowers engulfed in morning sunlight. Yoshinogawa,
Tokushima, Shikoku.

Two dandelions embrace in the warmth of the afternoon sun. Oshima Island, Tokyo.

Japanese calla flowers drenched by a torrential rain. The banks of the Kakita River, Mishima, Shizuoka Prefecture.

A bough of plum blossoms manifests its exquisite design
and beauty. Atami Plum Orchard, Shizuoka Prefecture.

Petal-laden branches of cherry blossoms caressed by
an evening breeze. Izu Peninsula, Shizuoka Prefecture.

Azalea flowers burgeoning next to a bamboo grove in the
hamlet of Shinden. Izu Peninsula, Shizuoka Prefecture.

A radiantly colourful cherry tree thrusts out above
the reflecting waters of Lake Okutama. Tokyo.

Sunlight streaming through low cloud formations
over the Sea of Japan. Atsuta Coast, Hokkaido.

A gathering storm above the waters of Lake Chuzenji.
Shafts of light dart through the overcast sky. Nikko
National Park, Tochigi Prefecture.

Ago Bay. Rafts and buoys create patterns on a
tranquil sea bathed in the sun's afterglow. Ise-Shima
National Park, Mie Prefecture.

At sundown on the beach at Kamakura, a small fishing boat is pushed out to sea for an evening catch. Kanagawa Prefecture.

麦立てて
あたり人なき
書き成す

ひとりきり
ねむ心や
雪を書く

六木

子明

夏

The oppressive heat of a summer day
My mind is whirling and whirling
As I listen to the distant peals of thunder.
　　　　　　　　—*Kyorai*

There is a fifth season in Japan—a mini-season—that lies between spring and summer. It is the monsoon season or *baiu*, which commences the first week in June and continues to mid-July.

This six-week period of precipitation is the fountain of life for rice crops throughout Japan; it keeps the rice paddies well supplied with water during the long, dry summer.

Hydrangeas and irises proliferate. Lotus flowers and water lilies too come into their own. Spring verdure fades to summer greens. By the time the monsoons subside, the sweltering heat of summer pervades the land.

During the scorching summer months, I often wonder how people coped with the unrelenting heat in days gone by. Reading the works of the haiku poets, one gets a sense of how unbearably hot it must have been.

But monsoons and muggy heat are only one aspect of the Japanese summer. There are fireworks displays, the voices of cicadas, the croaking of frogs at the edge of ponds and rice paddies. Bright paper lanterns hang everywhere during the O-bon festival, to welcome back the spirits of the deceased who are said to return to visit their families every summer. It is also the season to climb Mt. Fuji, when thousands of people of all ages make the arduous ascent to pay their respects to this towering symbol of Japan.

A discarded hoe standing in the paddy
Not a soul in sight
Oh! The brutal heat.
　　　　　　　　—*Shiki*

A field of barley undulates in the wind. Bibaushi
Village, Hokkaido.

Luminous summer clouds billow above verdant rice
paddies. Kaminoyama Village, Yamagata Prefecture.

A summer rice paddy
flourishes next to a
farmer's weather-beaten
hut. Kaminoyama,
Yamagata Prefecture.

Meandering rows of rice plants sprouting
through a rain-drenched paddy field.
Yokoyama Mountain, Ise-Shima,
Mie Prefecture.

A mountain trail winds
through a tunnel of
summer leafage.
Okunikkawa Village,
Miyagi Prefecture.

Iris flowers adorn the banks of a pond in the
garden of Heian Shrine. Kyoto.

Morning vapors waft across Odashiro Plateau. Nikko
National Park, Tochigi Prefecture.

Senjogahara at first light, its marshes veiled in morning
haze. Nikko National Park. Tochigi Prefecture.

The rising sun above Nantai Mountain bursts
through the morning fog. Nikko National Park.
Tochigi Prefecture.

Arasaki coast at dusk with the moon rising above
the horizon. Miura Peninsula, Kanagawa Prefecture.

Rape flowers grow in
abundance on the hills of
Naka-Furano. Hokkaido.

Solitary poppies blooming in the fields of
Kami-Furano. Hokkaido.

Dew drops embellish a spider's web amidst marsh plants on Senjogahara Plateau. Nikko National Park, Tochigi Prefecture.

Reeds sprouting in the Yukawa River, which flows across the Senjogahara Plateau. Nikko National Park, Tochigi Prefecture.

A golden sky above the mist-laden marshes of
Odashiro Plateau at daybreak. Nikko National Park,
Tochigi Prefecture.

The haze of a summer day still clings to mountain
slopes at dusk. The Japan Alps, Nagano Prefecture.

Rows of lavender contrast with barley fields on the
slopes of Kami-Furano. Hokkaido.

Lavish fields of wheat and flowers ornament the hills
of Naka-Furano. Hokkaido.

Stone Buddhist images
overlook a light-filled garden
of iris flowers. Ruins of
Mandarado, Zushi,
Kanagawa Prefecture.

Bamboo and maple bathed in early morning
light. Matsuo, Kyoto.

Sunlight shimmers on the
rushing waters of the
Oirase River. Towada,
Aomori Prefecture.

The plunging waters of Ashiribetsu Falls after
monsoon rains. Takino, Ishikari, Hokkaido.

A spider's web bejeweled with morning dew drops.
Senjogahara Plateau, Nikko National Park,
Tochigi Prefecture.

Prisms of light illuminate Shiraito Falls. In the
foreground, a summer tree in full flower. Itoshima,
Fukuoka Prefecture.

A becalmed sea off Manza
coast. A solitary boat and
single wave. Okinawa
Island.

A sea of clouds nestling in the valleys of
Irohazaka at the crack of dawn. Nikko
National Park, Tochigi Prefecture.

The red morning sky reflects on the waters of Oze Marsh. Fukushima Prefecture.

Markers pinpointing the location of oyster beds stick out from the shallow waters of Gokasho Bay. Ise-Shima, Mie Prefecture.

A spray of white lilies
under the silent eaves
of Kakuonji Temple.
Kamakura, Kanagawa
Prefecture.

Hydrangea flowers of Tokeiji Temple after
a rainy-season cloudburst. Kita-Kamakura,
Kanagawa Prefecture.

Hydrangea at Ajisai Temple not yet in full bloom. Kita-Kamakura, Kanagawa Prefecture.

Pink lilies in full flower. Yugashima, Izu Peninsula, Shizuoka Prefecture.

Biyoyanagi flowers on the hills above Yokosuka. Kanagawa Prefecture.

Water lilies floating on the pond of an ancient temple in Musashino. Tokyo.

AUTUMN

秋

On an autumn eve
There is a joy too
In man's loneliness.
                    —Buson

The Japanese archipelago stretches for over
2,000 miles from north to south, arching out
into the Pacific Ocean like a giant bow.
There is a latitudinal span of 15 degrees,
making for significant climatic variation and
bringing seasonal change early to some areas
and later to others.

   The first autumn tints manifest themselves
in early September in the northernmost parts
of Hokkaido, then gradually sweep down the
length of Japan over a three-month period.
Mountains, valleys, rivers, ravines, lakelands,
forests, marshes, plateaus, farmlands, rice
paddies, orchards and vineyards are all
caught up in this glorious progress.

   It is during this seasonal shift that each
region displays its own unique character. It is
the time of harvest and harvest festivals, a
time of ancient Shinto rites, thanking the
gods for abundant crops. It is a time of
changing moods and changing skies, a time
of cold winds and the harvest moon. And it
is a time of melancholy and sentimentality,
knowing autumn must fade and make way
for the icy grip of winter. Buson captures this
melancholy in his well known haiku.

In a short life
One hour is enough
This autumn night.
                    —Buson

A solitary mountain ash
tree, laden with ripe
berries. Togakushi Village,
Nagano Prefecture.

Branches of multicoloured maple overlook a
mountain stream on Aizu Plateau.
Fukushima Prefecture.

The main hall of Rinnoji Temple. Red and green
maple leaves backlit by the bright morning sun.
Nikko City, Tochigi Prefecture.

Sunlight filtering through the maple trees of Jingoji Temple.
The roof of the main hall is a harmonious backdrop.
Takao, Kyoto.

An overcast day in autumn. Rustic maple trees on
Kuriyama Mountain. Kinugawa, Tochigi Prefecture.

Fallen leaves carpet the roof of an ancient wooden
building at Sanzenin Temple. Ohara, Kyoto.

Dwindling days of autumn.
Sparse leaves and droplets
of water cling to the boughs
of a maple after torrential
rain. Atami Plum Orchard,
Shizuoka Prefecture.

Branches of autumn colours protrude over the
plunging waters of Ryuzu Falls. Nikko National
Park, Tochigi Prefecture.

Leafless silver birches standing as windbreakers on
the pastoral hills of Biei. Furano, Hokkaido.

Above the roof of Saimyoji Temple, maple leaves
and branches are disturbed by an evening breeze.
Takao Mountain, Kyoto.

A thicket of larch shimmering in slanting light.
On the mountainside at Takigahara, Nikko,
Tochigi Prefecture.

Larch, maple and cypress trees enliven the slopes
of Irohazaka with patterns of the season. Nikko
National Park, Tochigi Prefecture.

Branches of variegated
leaves create a delicate motif
of autumn. Hiraizumi,
Iwate Prefecture.

Fallen maple leaves rest on the stone
pathway of an ancient Shinto shrine.
Yamanaka Village, Ishikawa Prefecture.

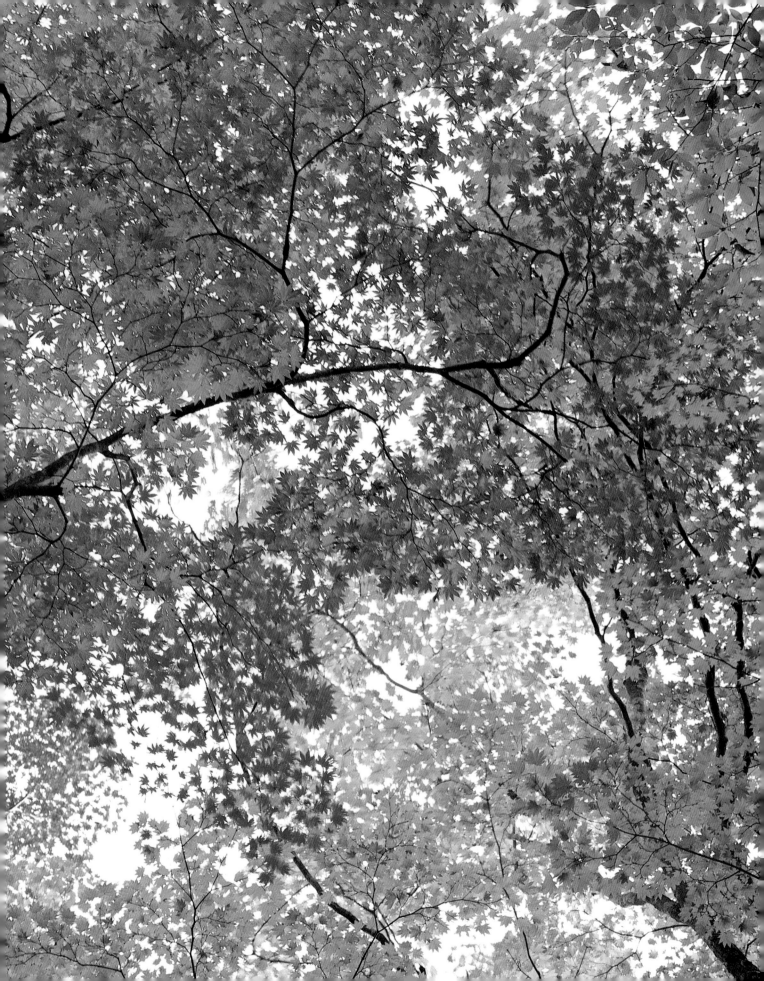

The sanctuary garden of Enkakuji Temple, carpeted
with fallen leaves. Kita-Kamakura, Kanagawa Prefecture.

Gingko leaves blanket the pathway leading to the
monks' quarters of an old Buddhist temple.
Kamakura, Kanagawa Prefecture.

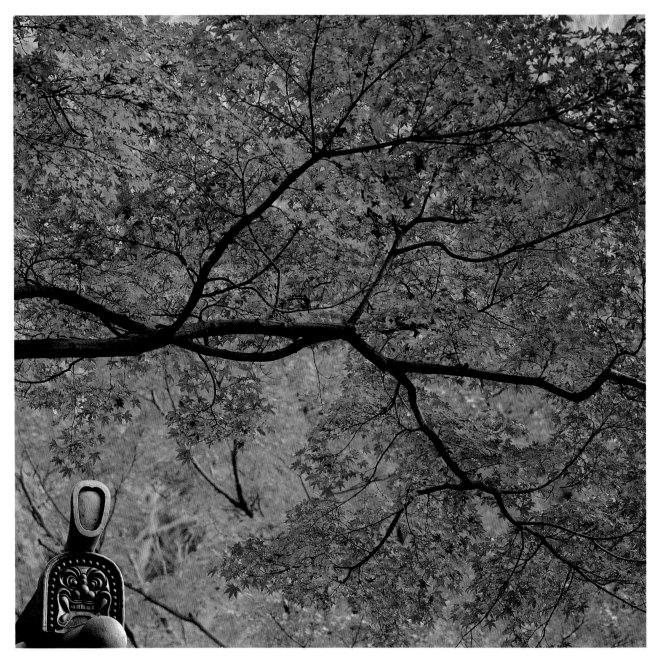

A fearsome rooftile on a temple gate is framed by
boughs of maples. Zuisenji Temple, Kamakura,
Kanagawa Prefecture.

The "Bamboo Temple" of Kamakura. Emerald green
trunks of bamboo are framed against a backdrop of
autumn hues. Kamakura, Kanagawa Prefecture.

Dawn bursts over the hills
north of Kyoto. Nomura
Village, Ohara, Kyoto.

Moments after sundown a solitary tree on the
horizon of Biei Hills is silhouetted against the
eventide sky. Furano, Hokkaido.

Elevated view of Zuisenji Temple.
In the foreground is the roof
of the main hall, and in the
distance the main gate. Kamakura,
Kanagawa Prefecture.

An ancient wall and an old maple tree create
a pattern of autumnal splendor. Kita-Kamakura,
Kanagawa Prefecture.

The sanctuary of Kakuonji Temple at dusk. Stone
Buddhist images are draped in red attire. Kamakura,
Kanagawa Prefecture.

The bell tower of Saimyoji Temple. Behind the bell,
a maple tree is bathed in morning sunlight. Takao
Mountain, Kyoto.

108

The flooded marsh of
Odashiro Plateau at dawn's
first light. Nikko National
Park, Tochigi Prefecture.

Autumn snow in a wooded area of Senjogahara
Plateau. The leaves of a solitary tree are still
green despite the early snowfall. Nikko
National Park, Tochigi Prefecture.

Late days of autumn. Wisps of foliage flutter in a
mountain gust. Kamikochi Valley, Nagano Prefecture.

The peak of Mount Manza shrouded in autumn fog.
Kusatsu, Gumma Prefecture.

Japanese *higanbana*, or
amaryllis, engulfed in
tremulous light.
Mount Narita, Chiba
Prefecture.

Cosmos flowers surround a stone lantern at
Enkyuji Temple. Kamakura,
Kanagawa Prefecture.

Harvested rice hanging out to dry. To the rear of the field, prolific pampas grass creates a harmonious scene of texture and colors. Naruko Village, Miyagi Prefecture.

A rice paddy after heavy rain. On the bank of the paddy, Japanese *higanbana* is in full bloom. Ohara, Kyoto.

Onions hanging out to dry are a sure sign of autumn's arrival. Zao Village, Yamagata Prefecture.

An ancient bell tower is utilized to dry persimmons for the winter months. Noto Peninsula, Ishikawa Prefecture.

Corns of cob hanging out to dry in the autumn sun. Togakushi Village, Nagano Prefecture.

Red peppers drying against a thatched mountain hut. Aizu Wakamatsu, Fukushima Prefecture.

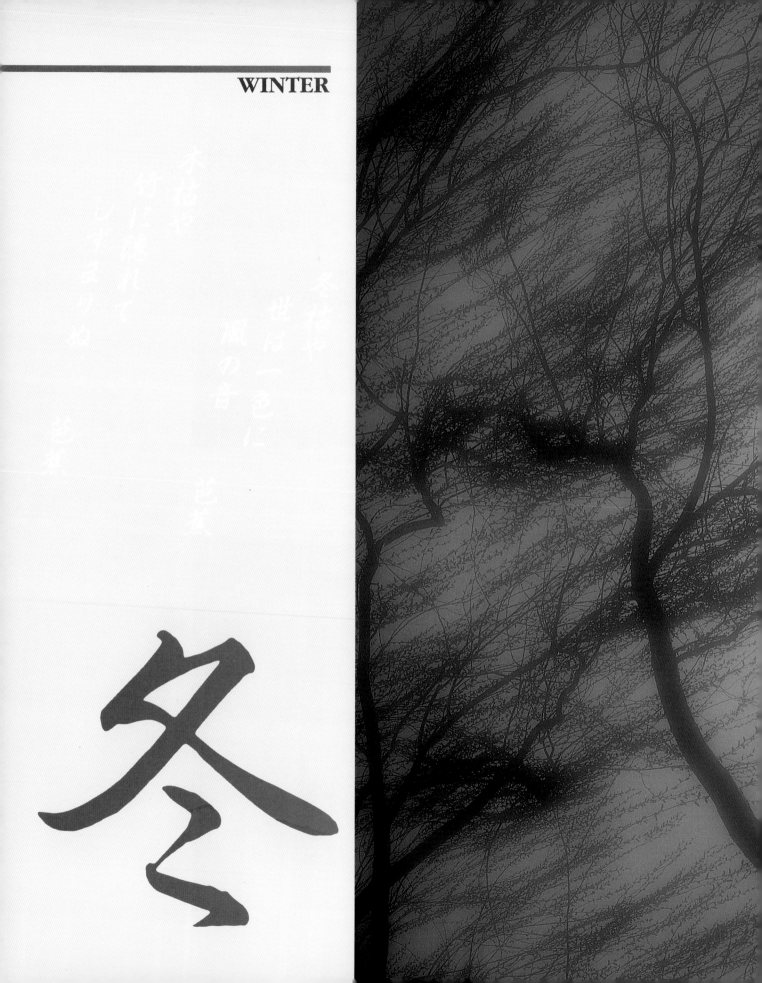

冬枯や
世は一色に
風の音

芭蕉

木枯や
竹に隠れて
しづまりぬ

芭蕉

冬

The desolation of winter
In a world of one colour
Assailed by a wailing wind.
　　　　—Basho

Northern Japan has an extremely harsh
winter. Cold air masses from Siberia pick up
moisture as they cross the Sea of Japan,
which they deposit as rain or snow over the
Japanese islands. When this climatic change
manifests itself, winter begins in earnest.

The first snows fall in northwest Honshu
and Hokkaido in November, and these areas
remain under snow until the beginning of
April. Inhabitants of the more isolated regions
stock up with provisions before the first
blizzards strike.

The Sea of Okhotsk and Shiretoko Peninsula freeze over, resembling the ice flows of
the Arctic. Temperatures stay at subzero for
weeks. The Hokkaido brown bear and the
Honshu Tsukinowa bear go into hibernation;
wild deer and foxes forage for food, not
always surviving.

Mountains attract skiers and alpinists,
some of whom die in atrocious, unpredictable
weathers. Truly, the Japanese winter of the
deep north is a thing to be respected.

Many of the old villages in the north have
existed in the snow country for centuries and
know well the mean spirit of winter and her
perverse unrelenting ways. Survival has never
been taken lightly here.

They say that the reason the inhabitants of
Aomori speak with a dialect unintelligible to
anyone else is that they prefer not to open
their mouths too wide in the bitter, piercing
winds. Perhaps it was in these same ancient
villages that the haiku poets of yesteryear
observed the season's capriciousness.

The winter tempest
Hid itself in the bamboos
And grew still.
　　　　—Basho

Todowara marshlands
moments after sundown.
The winter temperature has
dropped to minus 30°C.
Notsuke Peninsula,
Hokkaido.

Fishing nets hang in the solitude of a partially
frozen lake. Onuma Quasi-Prefectural Park,
Hokkaido.

The frozen banks of the
meandering Ku hiro River
reflect the vivid colours of
an intense afterglow.
Kushiro Marsh, Hokkaido.

Early morning hoarfrost forms a winter
pattern on top of a barren rice paddy.
Togakushi Village, Nagano Prefecture.

Senjogahara Plateau in the early evening. A new
moon shines through the clear winter sky. Nikko
National Park, Tochigi Prefecture.

Okinawa in December. A lustrous evening sky sweeps
out above the coast of Manza. Okinawa Island.

The setting sun above desolate farmland. An abandoned hayrake lies half-buried in the frozen snow. Notsuke Peninsula, Hokkaido.

The roof of Nishi-Honganji Temple and its encompassing trees are silhouetted against the afterglow of a cold winter sky. Kyoto.

A deserted beach. The rays of the setting sun transform the icy waves into warm golden hues. Katsurakoi Village, Kushiro, Hokkaido.

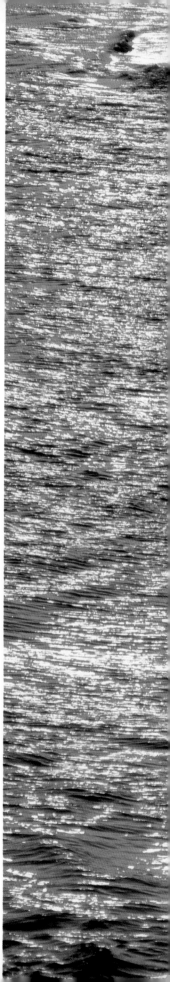

A single-track railway bends and curves into the rays of the setting sun. Kayanuma, Kushiro Marsh, Hokkaido.

Bundles of rice straw hanging outside a store-house for winter. The straw is used for many purposes, including protection against the harsh winter elements. Hakuba, Nagano Prefecture.

Hakuba Village during a blizzard. The woman in the distance is carrying her baby through the icy wind and snow. Northern Japan Alps, Nagano Prefecture.

A tributary of the Kushiro River, its banks partially
frozen into a winter portrait of glacial beauty.
Kushiro Marsh, Hokkaido.

A large tree festooned with frost flakes during the
bite of mid-winter. Chanokidaira Plateau, Nikko
National Park, Tochigi Prefecture.

The eaves of Nikko's five-storied pagoda and the surrounding cedars are cloaked in the first snow of winter. Nikko City, Tochigi Prefecture.

The bamboo garden of Hokokuji Temple after a snow flurry. The bamboo looks particularly lovely with snow clinging to its slender boughs. Kamakura, Kanagawa Prefecture.

A large Japanese plum tree
bedecked with the first
snow of winter. Onocho
Village, Oshima, Southern
Hokkaido.

The turbulent Sea of Japan in late December.
Forbidding storm clouds gather on the
horizon, off the rugged coastline of Sado
Island. Niigata Prefecture.

Freshly fallen snow has melted on top of the ice at
Tashiro Pond. Kamikochi Valley, Nagano Prefecture.

The first winter snow cloaks Taisho Pond in
Kamikochi Valley. Nagano Prefecture.

The jagged, rocky shores of Arasaki during a winter gale.
This coastal region is spectacularly beautiful on stormy
days. Miura Peninsula, Kanagawa Prefecture.

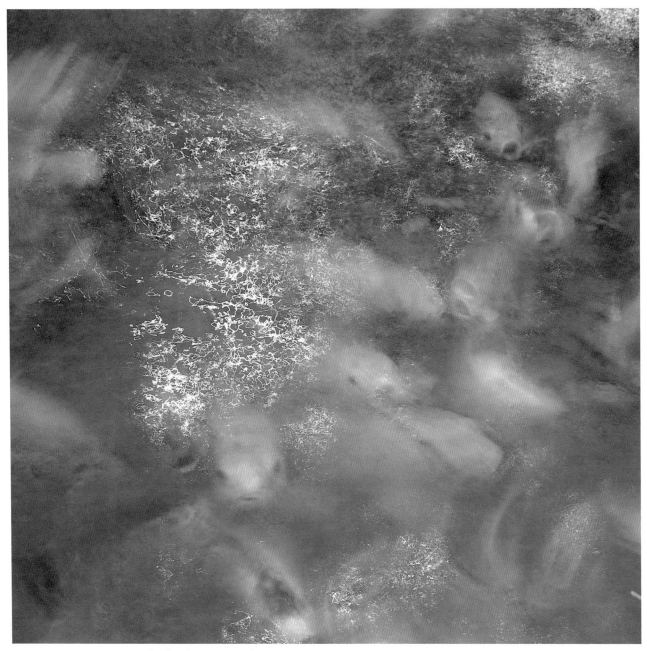

Japanese carp congregate for feeding time in the
pond of Tenryuji Temple. Arashiyama, Kyoto.

Early winter snow covers the maple trees at Lake
Chuzenji, combining both autumn and winter into
one scene. Nikko National Park, Tochigi Prefecture.

A flooded barren rice paddy reflects the glow of a
cold winter sun at daybreak. Fukuroda Village,
Ibaraki Prefecture.

Homemade Japanese rice-cakes being dried in the cold
winter air, for use during the New Year festivities.
Hinoemata Village, Fukushima Prefecture.

Small pleasure boats at Lake Kizaki are stored for
the winter. The lake is frozen over from late
December to March. Nagano Prefecture.

The main hall of Rinnoji Temple. A snow-covered tree in the foreground evokes a pattern of winter harmony. Nikko, Tochigi Prefecture.

Shinkyo, the sacred red bridge of Nikko, during a
late winter snowfall. Nikko, Tochigi Prefecture.

Hawthorn berries blanketed with the first snow of
winter. Tokura, Nagano Prefecture.

A desolate *torii* gate lies half-buried in the snow. The
small hamlet of Sawado. Hakuba, Nagano Prefecture.

The frost-laden marshes of Odashiro Plateau in mid-winter. Nikko National Park, Tochigi Prefecture.

The pastoral fields of Biei on a bitterly cold
morning in November. Winter in this region can be
extremely harsh. Furano, Hokkaido.

Nature never did betray the heart that loved her.

William Wordsworth
1770-1850